Juneteenth

A celebration

Written by: Courtney Juste

Illustrated by: Silver Star

Acknowledgments:

A special thank you to the love of my life Ronald for being my adventure partner, cheerleader, and fellow freedom fighter. I would also like to thank the many mommies on the liberation front that teach me, uplift me and understand me when it seems no one else does.

Printed in the United States of America

First Printing, 2021
ISBN 978-1-7373876-1-9

Library of Congress Control Number: 2021912539

This book is dedicated to my dearest Mandela Rose and all of generation alpha.

May you live as freely and liberated as possible.

This book is also an offering to my ancestors known and unknown that guide me everyday.

When America began
the colonizers
enslaved African teachers,
doctors, and farmers to
work for free in
cotton and tobacco fields.

Atlantic
Ocean

Passage

West
Africa

Former citizens of an area now known as Benin had many of its citizens taken away in chains.

Benin

Before leaving their homes, Beninese women were very creative. They hid rice seeds in their braids before being forced onto ships.

These brilliant women made sure that their families had food to make the journey to an unknown and scary place.

Several foods that we enjoy today including okra, mac and cheese, rice, and black-eyed peas all came onto the shores of the United States with enslaved Africans.

One of America's most popular instruments, the banjo, was a remake of a stringed instrument called the akonting from West Africa.

The banjo wouldn't exist without the brain power and craftsmanship of Africans.

As enslaved people,
they could not stop working
even if they were tired.

They built houses and bridges, planted and harvested crops, and cooked meals for others every day.

This cruel and unfair system made the United States lots of money for over 340 years.

Tired of being mistreated, brave women and men revolted or escaped at night.

They gave speeches about their horrible experiences and risked their lives to share their stories.

Some citizens wanted to keep the institution of slavery, but the abolitionists said **NO!**

In the year **1863** the President used lots of big words in a speech called the Emancipation Proclamation.

His words declared
the **4** Million enslaved
African-Americans as free.

BUT since they did not have TVs,
telephones, or the internet
like we do now;

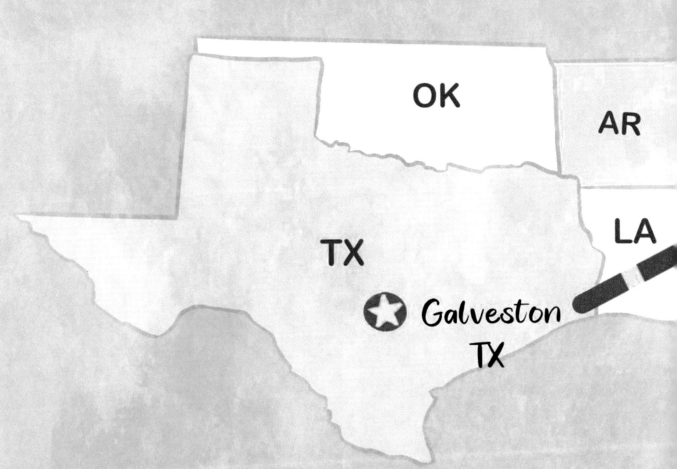

OK

AR

TX

LA

★ Galveston
TX

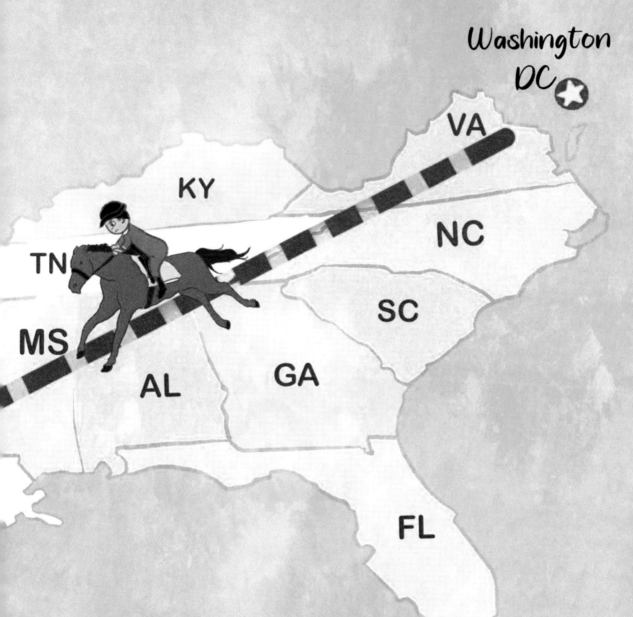

Washington DC ★

VA

KY

NC

TN

SC

MS

GA

AL

FL

it took a loooooong time
for the news to reach Texas
from Washington D.C.

It took two years for
the 2000 federal soldiers
to reach the state of Texas.

On June 19th, 1865 they walked the streets of Galveston and shared news of the end of chattel slavery in America.

Exactly one year later,
June 19th, 1866 Galveston's black
citizens gathered to remember
the day they were emancipated
or freed from bondage.

Creatively they combined the name of the month June with the number date Nineteenth to create a new holiday called Juneteenth!

After being denied education,
black citizens all over America
created their own schools,
started businesses,
and ran for political offices.

And every year they met on Juneteenth to party as a community.

Juneteenth parties include food, music, family and friends in parks around the country.

Many, many years after the first Juneteenth, someone created a special flag to remember the day.

The star on the Juneteenth flag is like the star on the Texas state flag because Texas is where the holiday started.

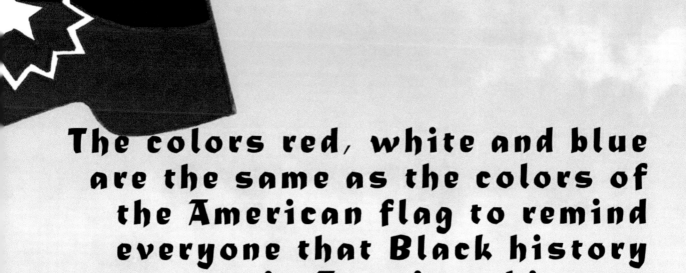

The colors red, white and blue are the same as the colors of the American flag to remind everyone that Black history is American history.

Barbecue, red soda, and watermelon were served at some of the first Juneteenth celebrations.

The color red reminds those participating of the bloodshed by those who fought for freedom.

Some cities have parades and Ms. Juneteenth pageants as well.

On this day we feel love, joy, happiness and pride in all the accomplishments that our Black American ancestors have made.

It's Juneteenth! A celebration.

Made in United States
Orlando, FL
25 May 2022

18163703R00024